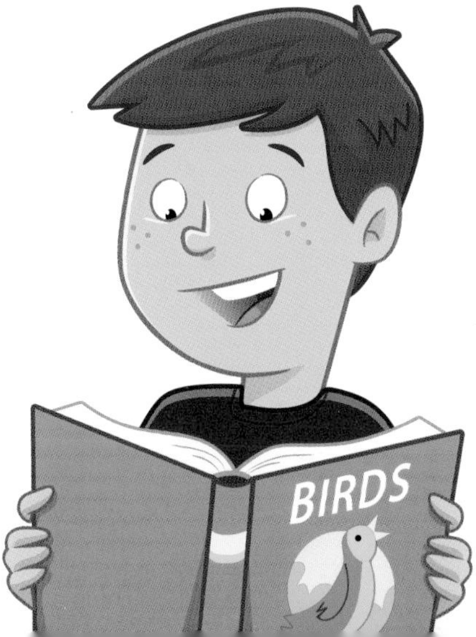
BIRDS

# WHERE DO THE BIRDS GO?

## A MIGRATION MYSTERY

Haverstraw King's Daughters
Public Library
10 W. Ramapo Rd.
Garnerville, NY 10923

BY REBECCA OLIEN

ILLUSTRATED BY KATIE M<sup>C</sup>DEE

CONSULTANT:

David Stokes, PhD
Associate Professor
Interdisciplinary Arts and Sciences
University of Washington, Bothell

CAPSTONE PRESS
a capstone imprint

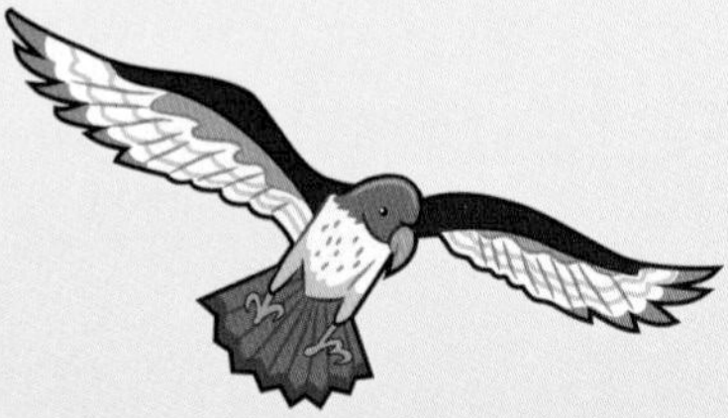

First Graphics are published by Capstone Press,
151 Good Counsel Drive, P.O. Box 669, Mankato, Minnesota 56002.
www.capstonepub.com



Books published by Capstone Press are manufactured with paper containing at least 10 percent post-consumer waste.

*Library of Congress Cataloging-in-Publication Data*
Olien, Rebecca.
Where do the birds go? : a migration mystery / by Rebecca Olien ; illustrated by Katie McDee.
p. cm.—(First graphics. Science mysteries)
Includes bibliographical references and index.
Summary: "In graphic novel format, text and illustrations explain why birds migrate"—Provided by publisher.
ISBN 978-1-4296-6096-9 (library binding)
ISBN 978-1-4296-7175-0 (paperback)
1. Birds—Migration—Juvenile literature. 2. Migratory birds—Juvenile literature. I. McDee, Katie, ill. II. Title.
QL698.9.O45 2012
598.156'8—dc22 2011001014

EDITOR: CHRISTOPHER L. HARBO
DESIGNER: LORI BYE
ART DIRECTOR: NATHAN GASSMAN
PRODUCTION SPECIALIST: ERIC MANSKE

Printed in the United States of America in Stevens Point, Wisconsin.
032011 006111WZF11

# TABLE OF CONTENTS

# What Is Migration?

Some birds don't live in one place all year. In the fall, many birds fly to warmer places.

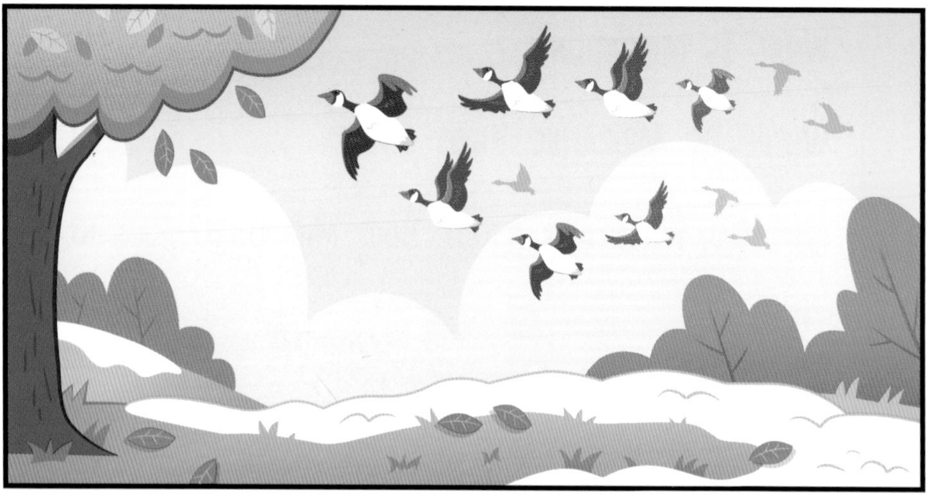

In the spring, these birds return to their summer homes.

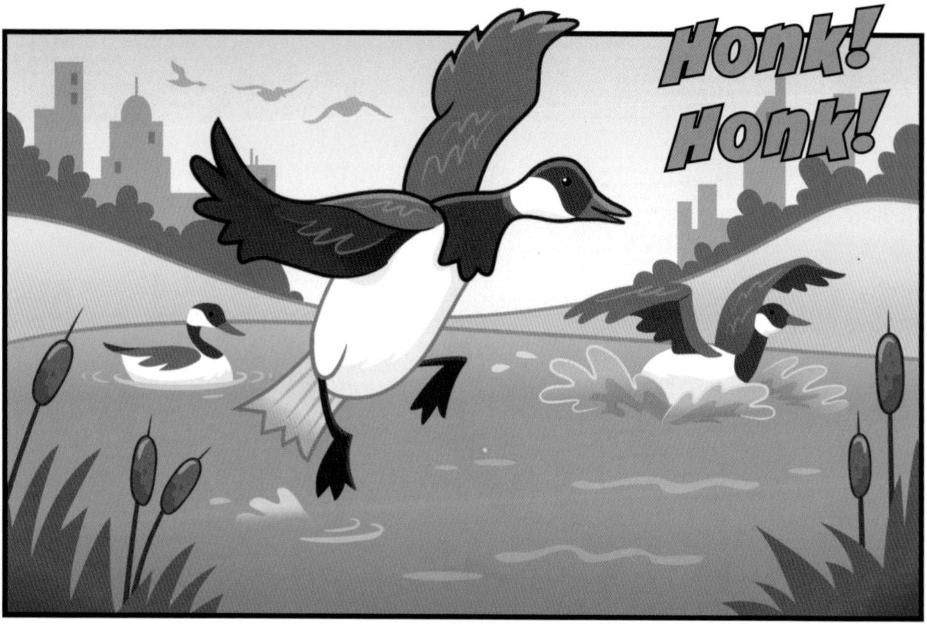
Honk!
Honk!

This seasonal movement is called migration.

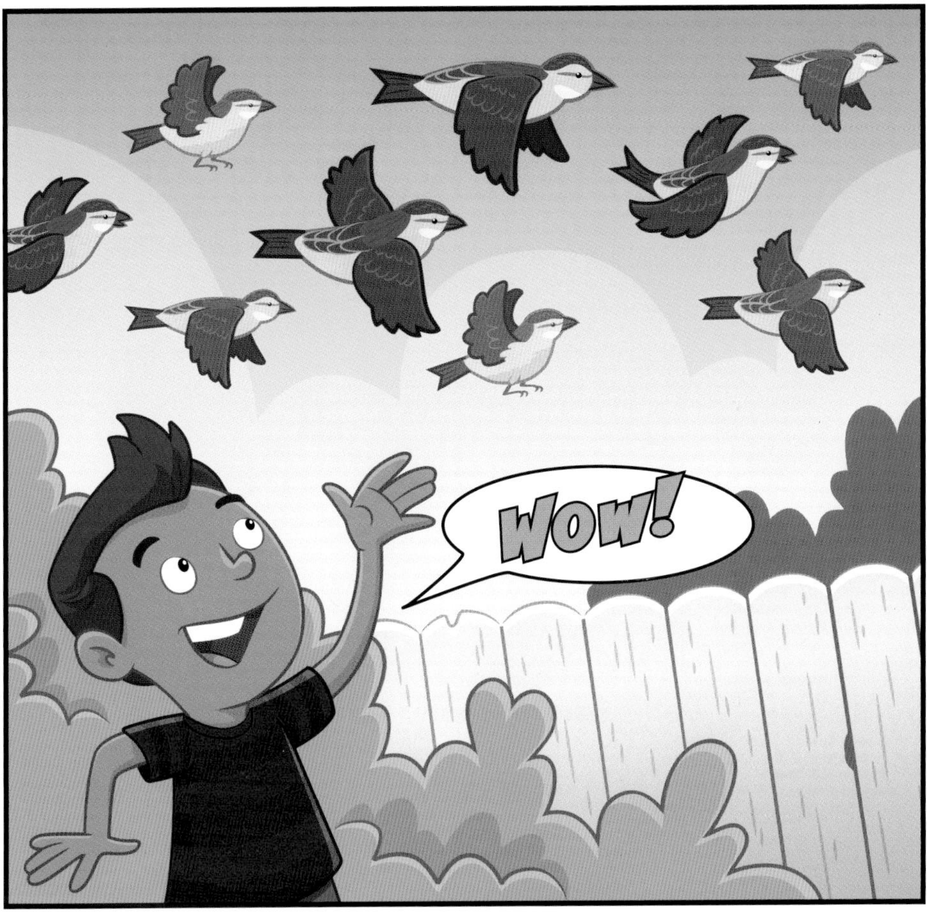
WOW!

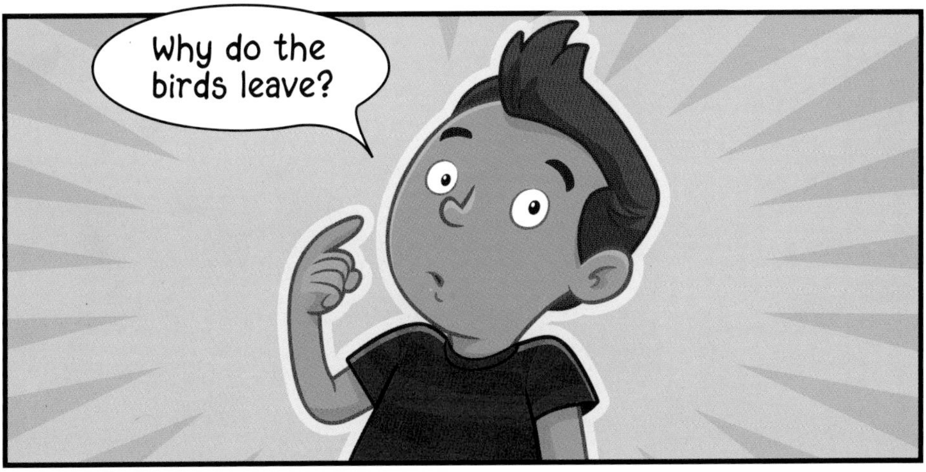
Why do the birds leave?

In the winter, ducks can't find food through the ice on lakes. Some songbirds can't find the berries and bugs they eat.

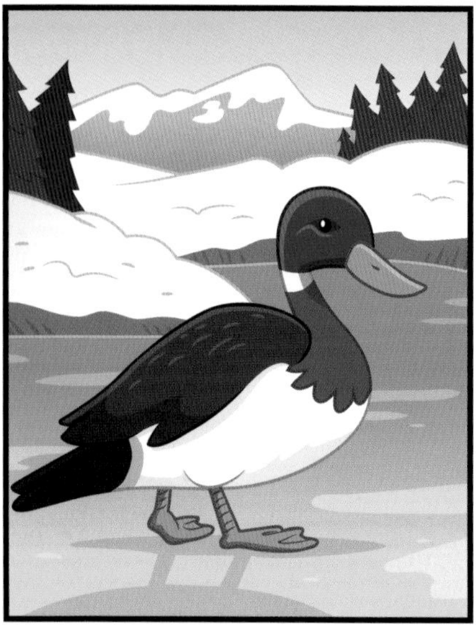

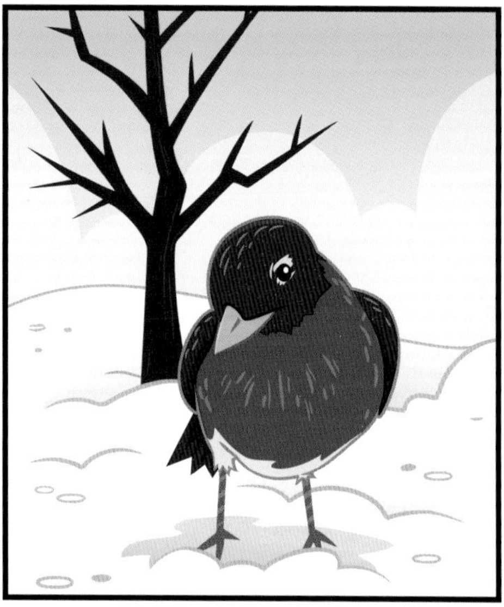

Some hawks can't find the small animals they hunt.

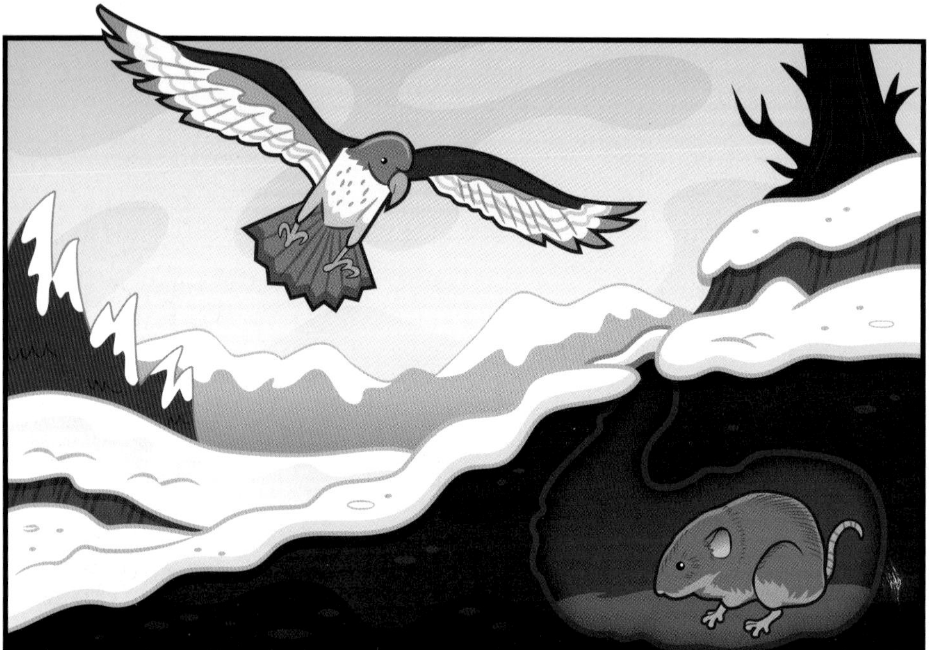

All of these birds migrate to warmer places where food is easier to find.

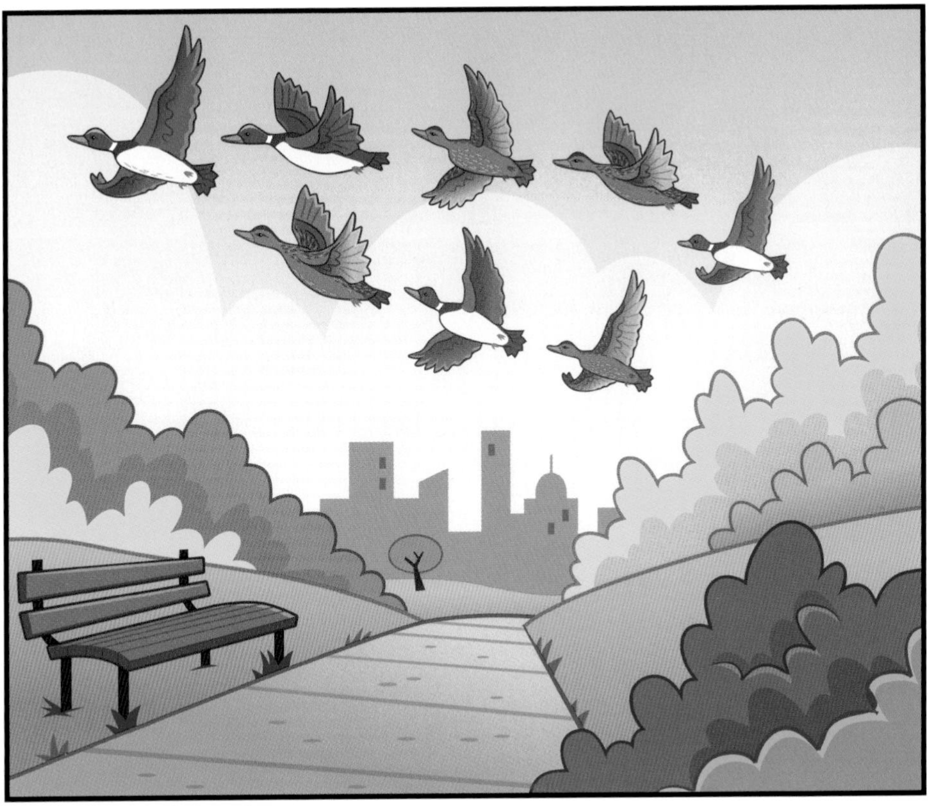

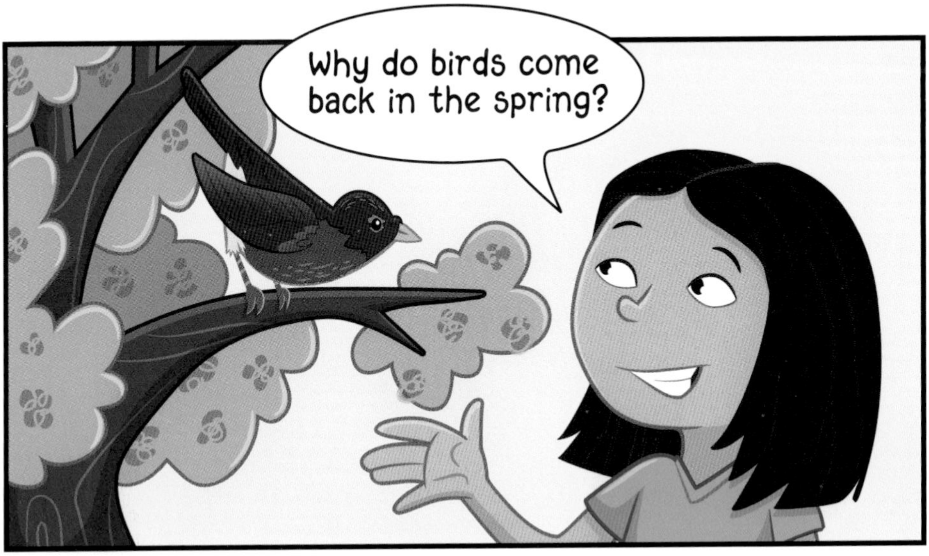
Why do birds come back in the spring?

Birds return in the spring to have young.

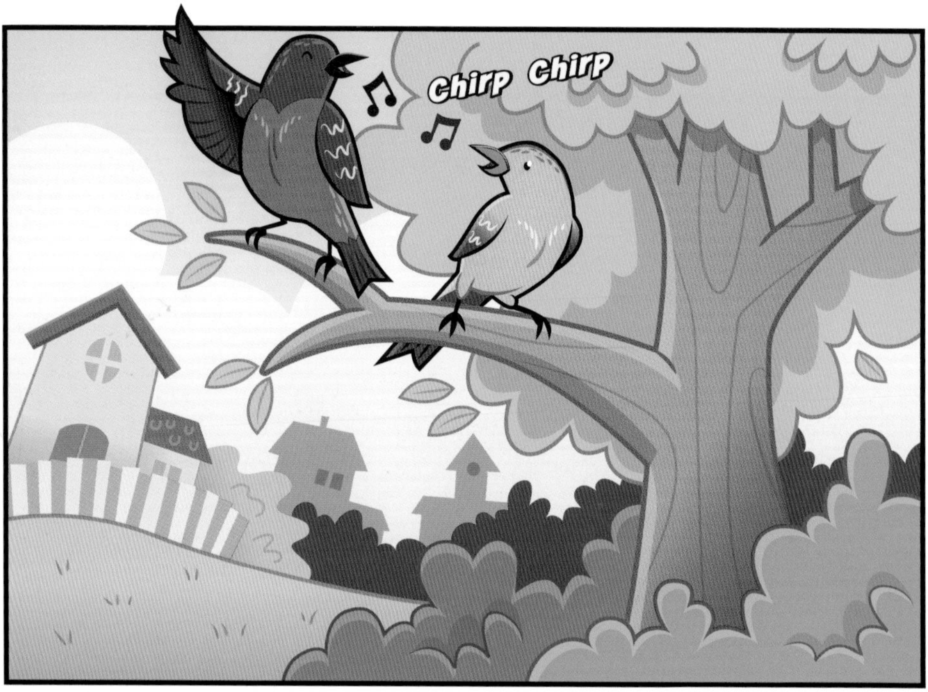
Chirp Chirp

They build nests to lay their eggs.

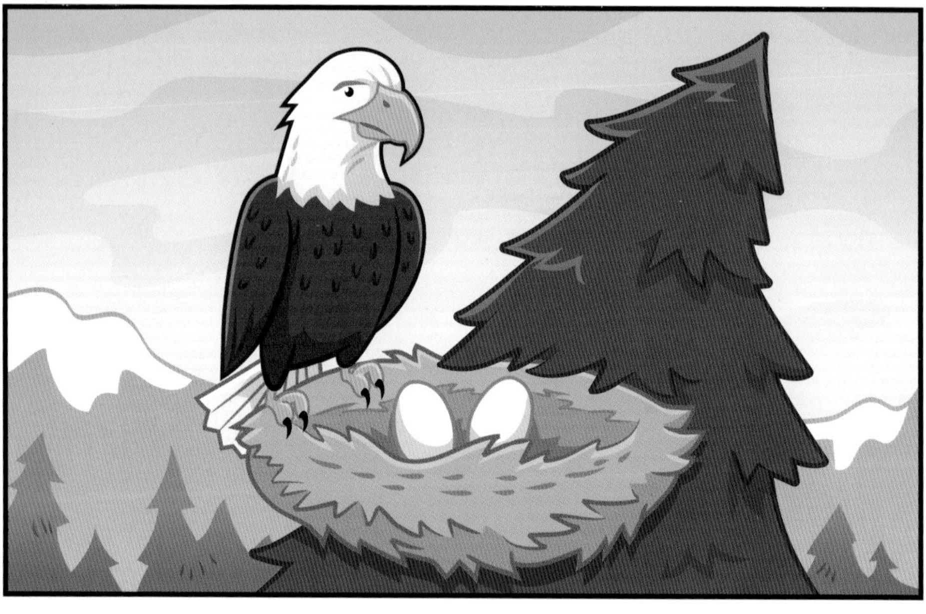

They care for their young all summer.

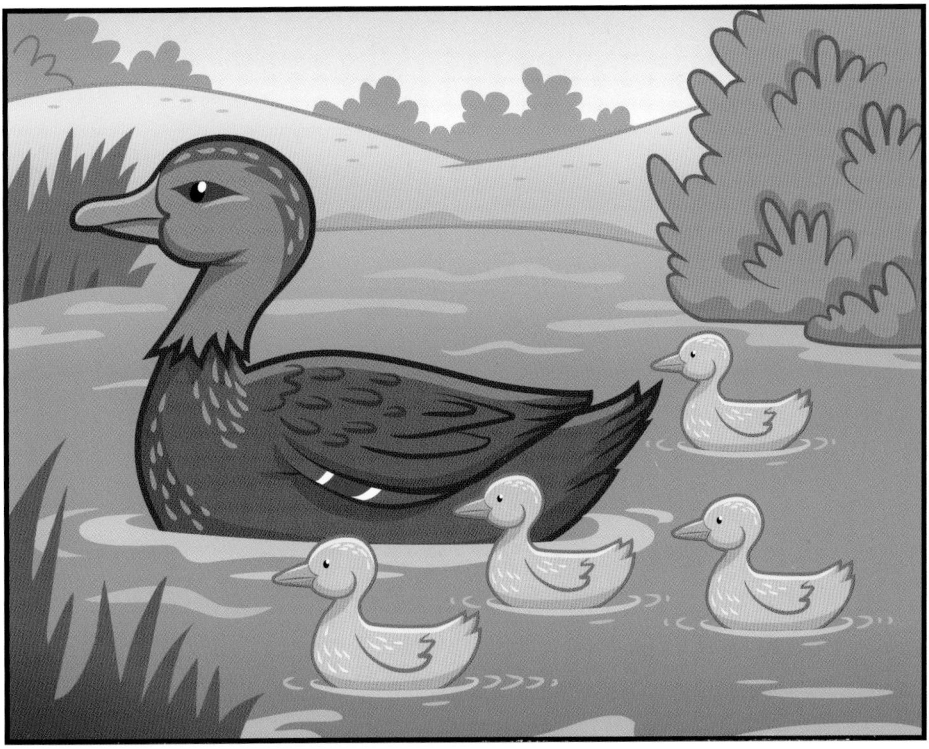

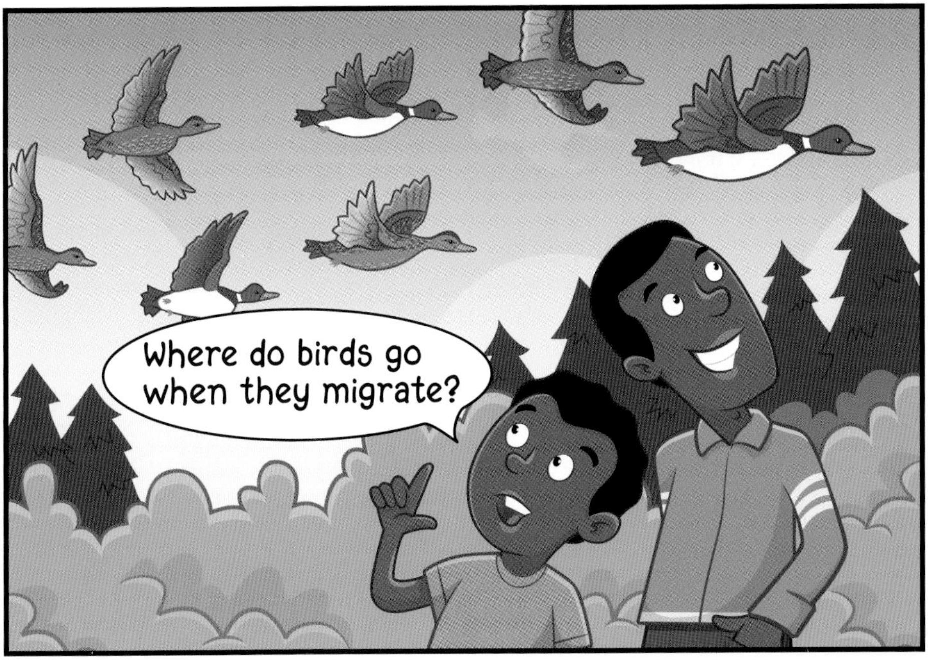
Where do birds go when they migrate?

# Where Do Migrating Birds Go?

Birds migrate to many parts of the world.

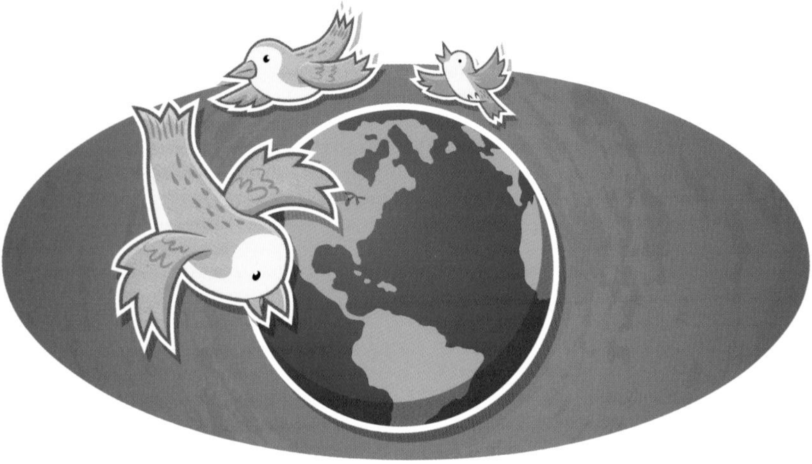

The arctic tern travels from one end of Earth to the other.

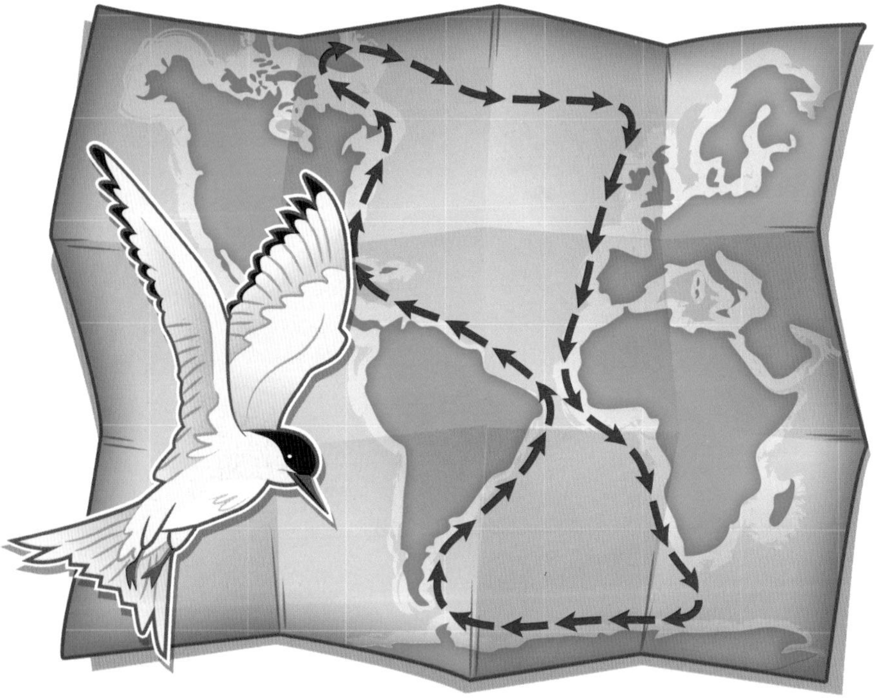

California gulls fly to the Pacific Ocean in the fall. They return to their nesting grounds in the spring.

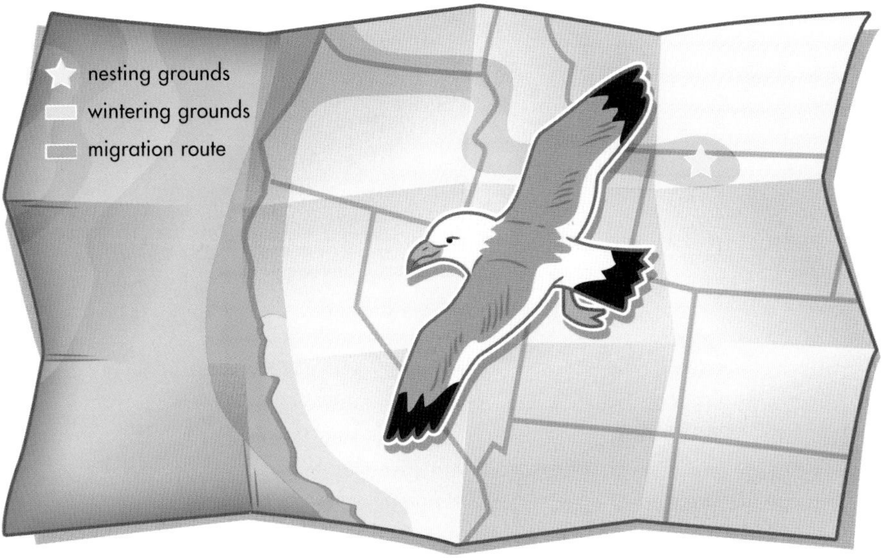
nesting grounds
wintering grounds
migration route

Even tiny hummingbirds migrate. Some travel from Alaska to Mexico and back again.

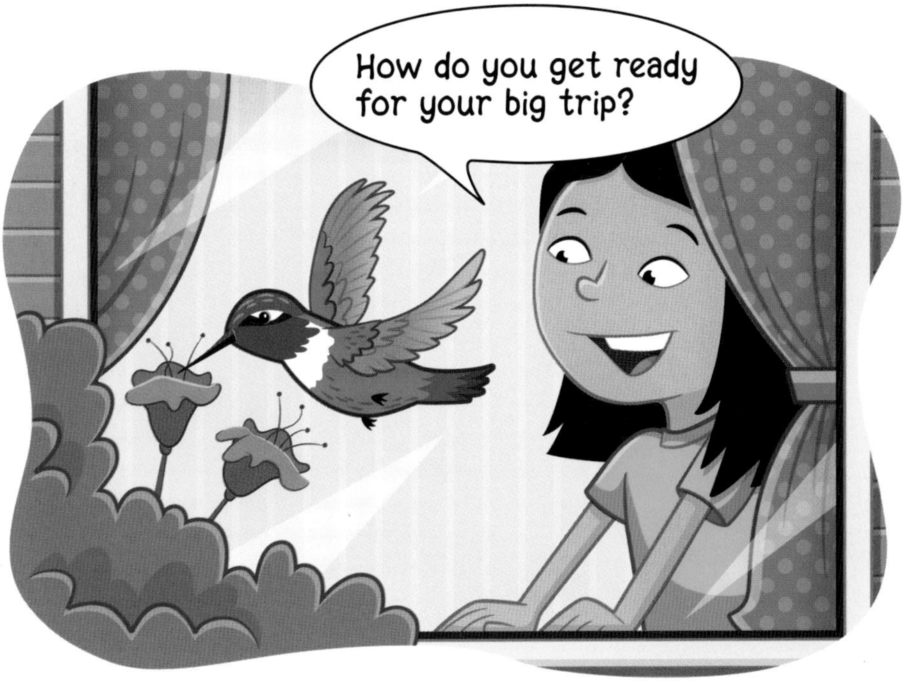
How do you get ready for your big trip?

People get ready to take a long trip. Birds do too.

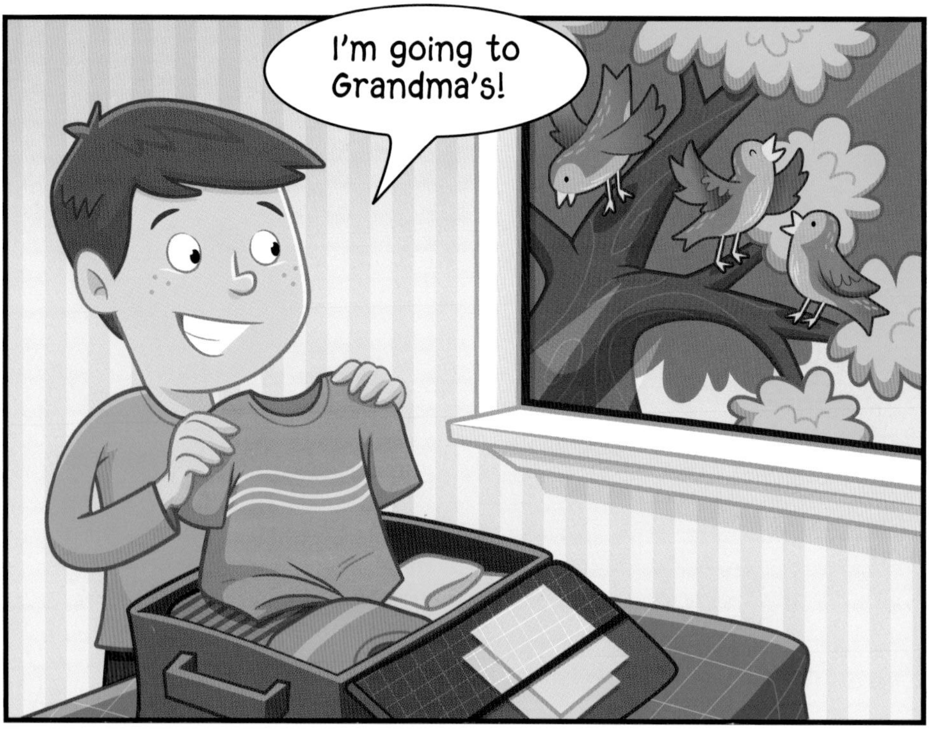
I'm going to Grandma's!

Many birds grow new feathers to help them fly.

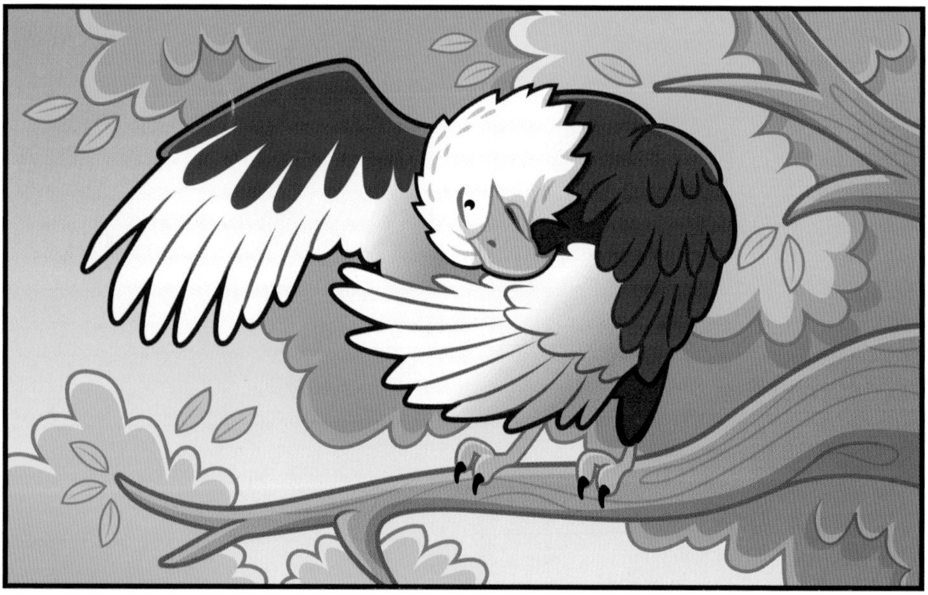

Birds eat a lot before they migrate. Food gives them energy to fly.

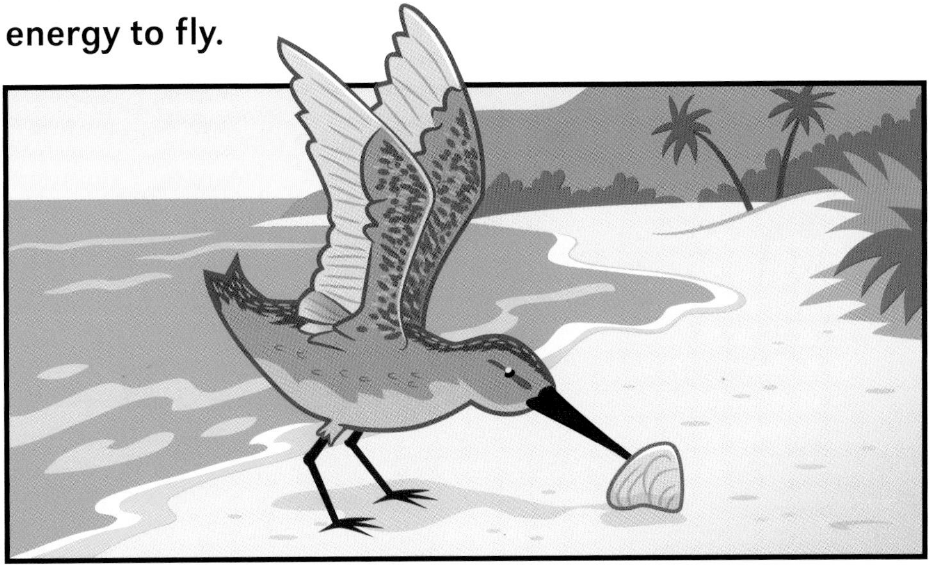

Some birds travel in flocks to migrate. Flying together is safer than flying alone.

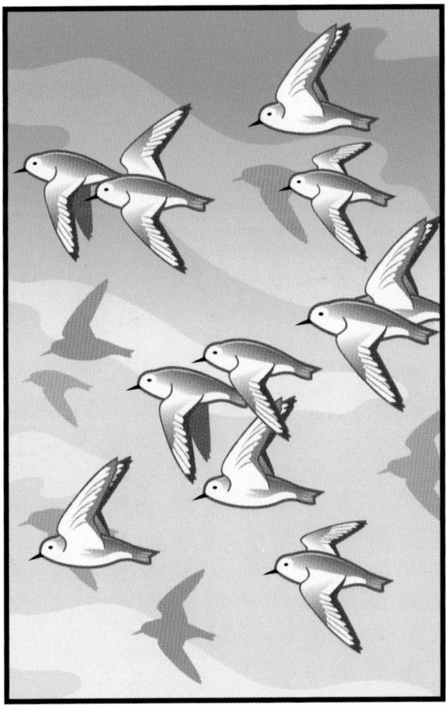

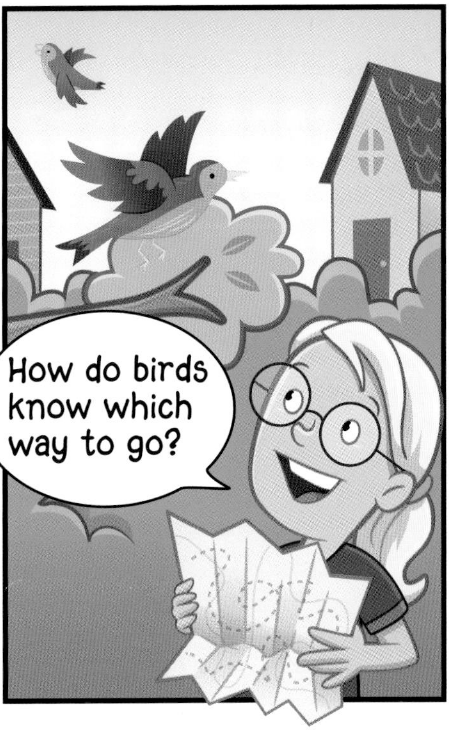
How do birds know which way to go?

Most birds migrate at night. They use the stars to guide them.

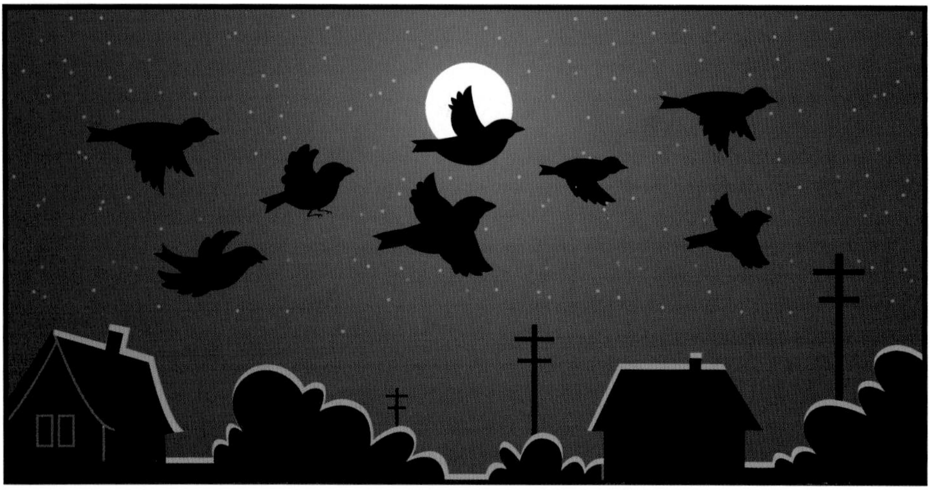

Birds flying by day use the sun. They also follow landmarks such as rivers, mountains, and coasts.

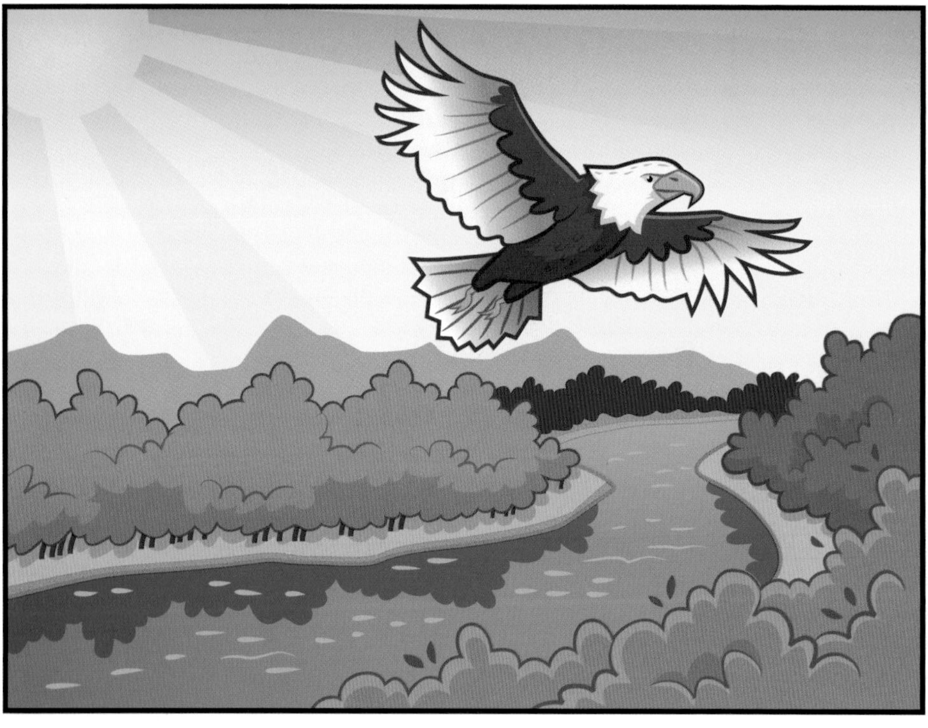

Earth acts like a big magnet. It has a magnetic field that birds can sense.

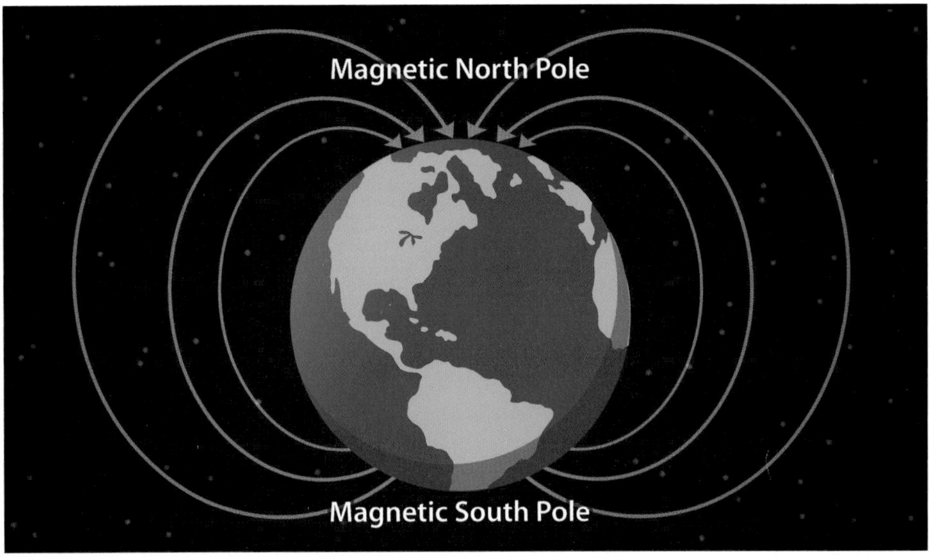
Magnetic North Pole
Magnetic South Pole

The magnetic field helps birds fly in the right direction.

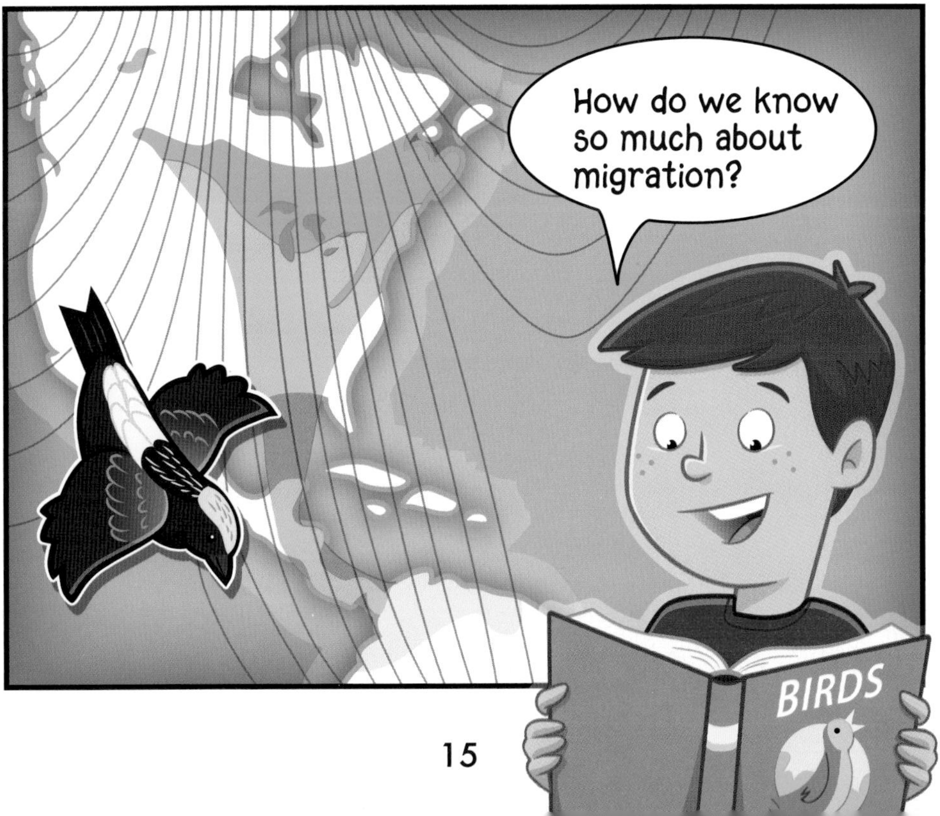
How do we know so much about migration?
BIRDS

# How Do We Learn about Bird Migration?

Bird banders help scientists learn about migration.

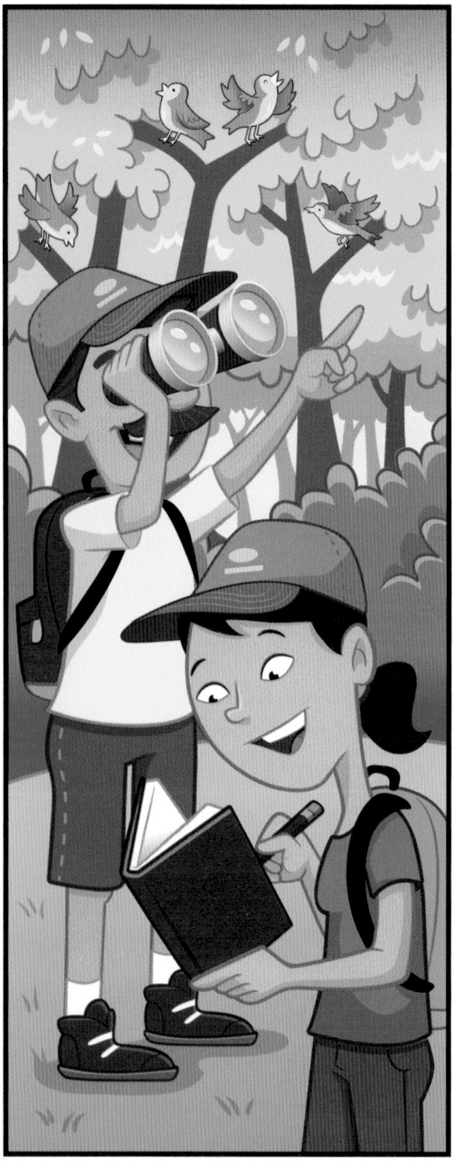

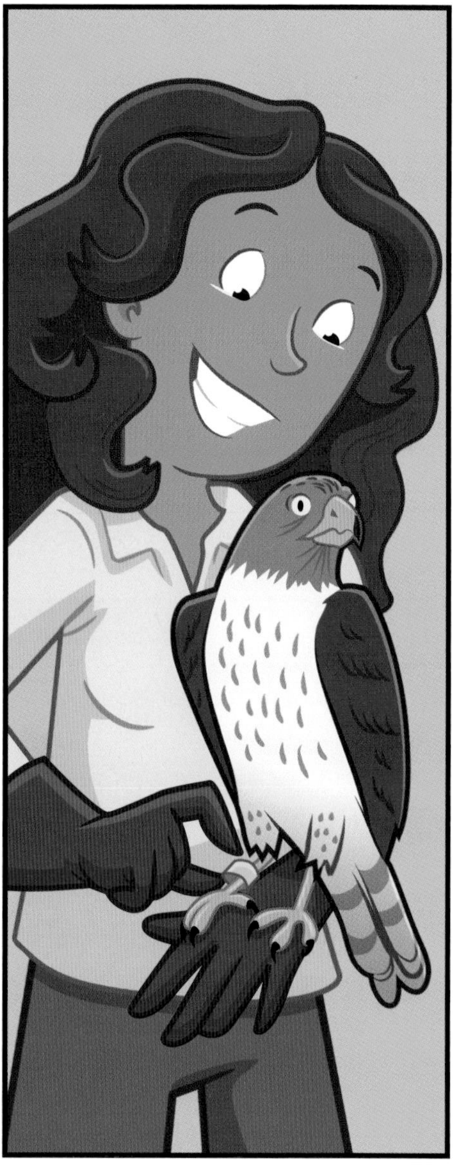

Bird banders catch birds safely. They put numbered bands around the birds' legs.

The band number shows where the bird came from.

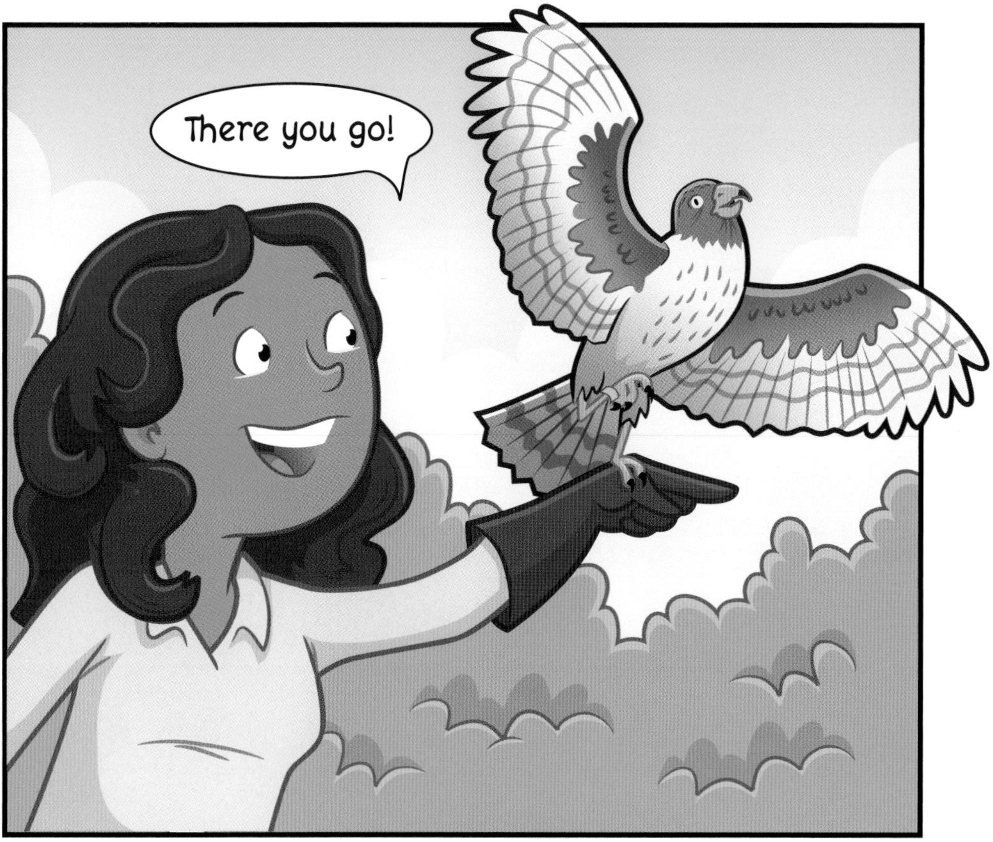
There you go!

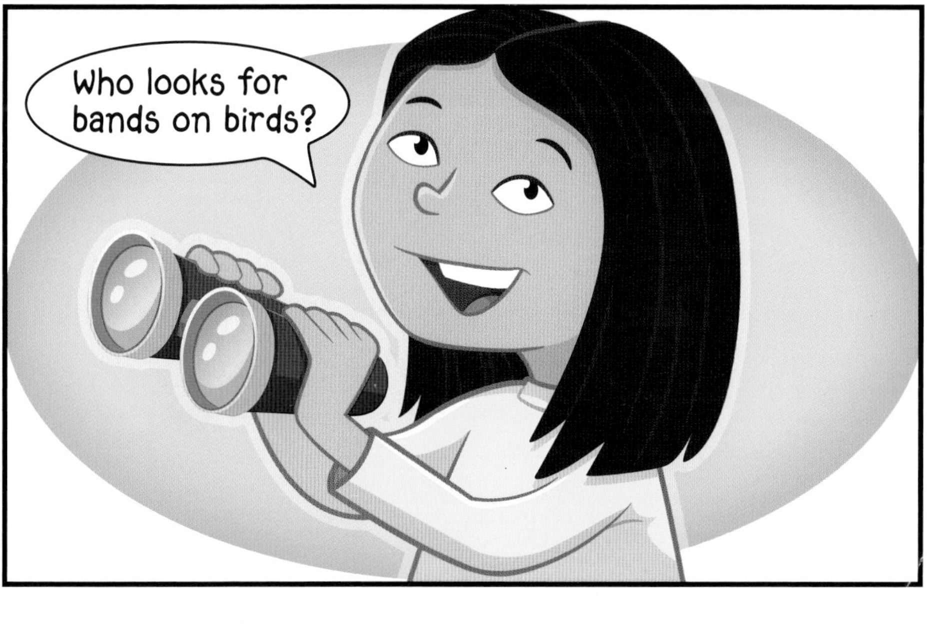
Who looks for bands on birds?

Bird watchers look for banded birds.

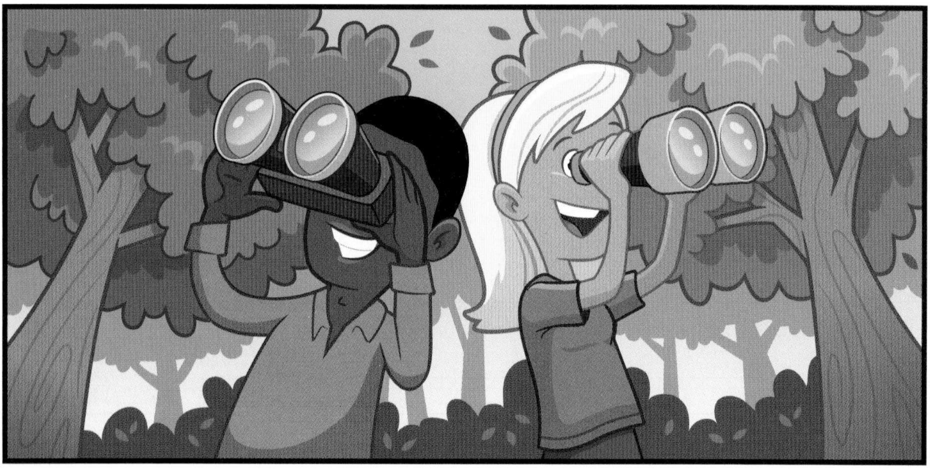

Bird watchers write down when and where they see birds. They share their notes with scientists.

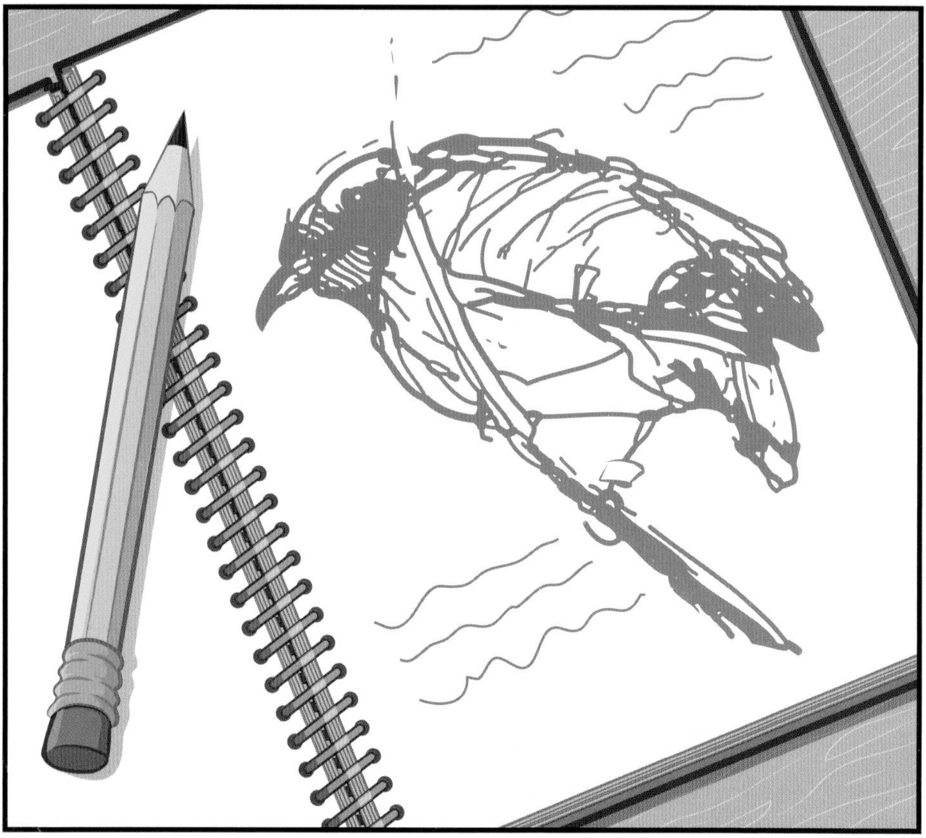

This information helps scientists learn when and where birds migrate.

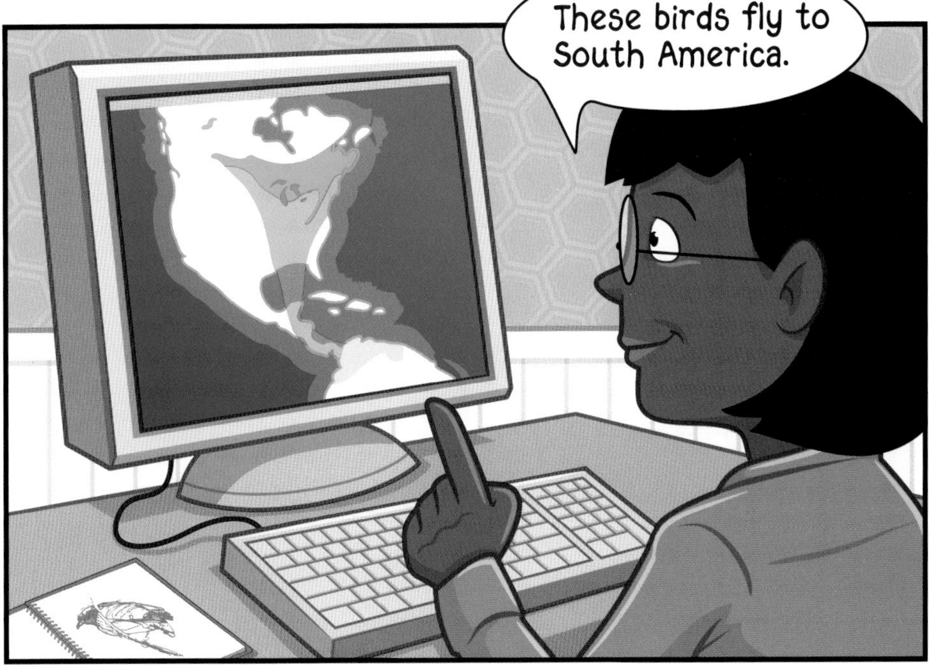
These birds fly to South America.

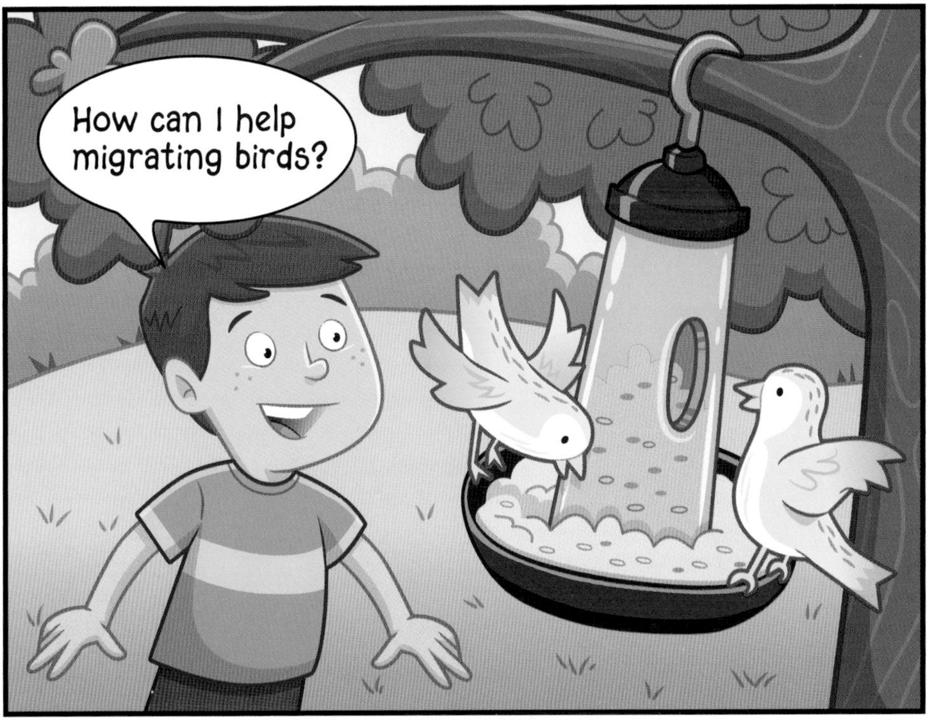
How can I help migrating birds?

Some birds use trees for shelter during migration. You can help by planting trees.

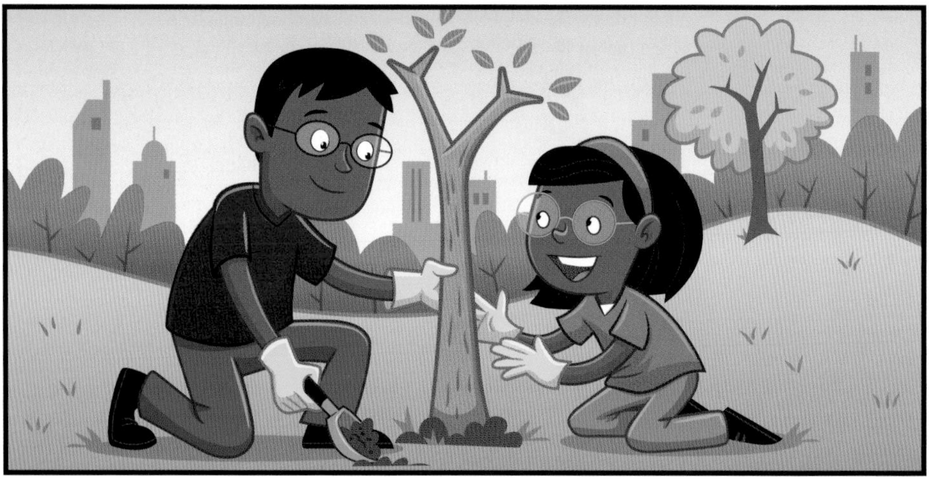

Pets catch birds that are tired from long flights. Protect birds by keeping pets indoors or on a leash.

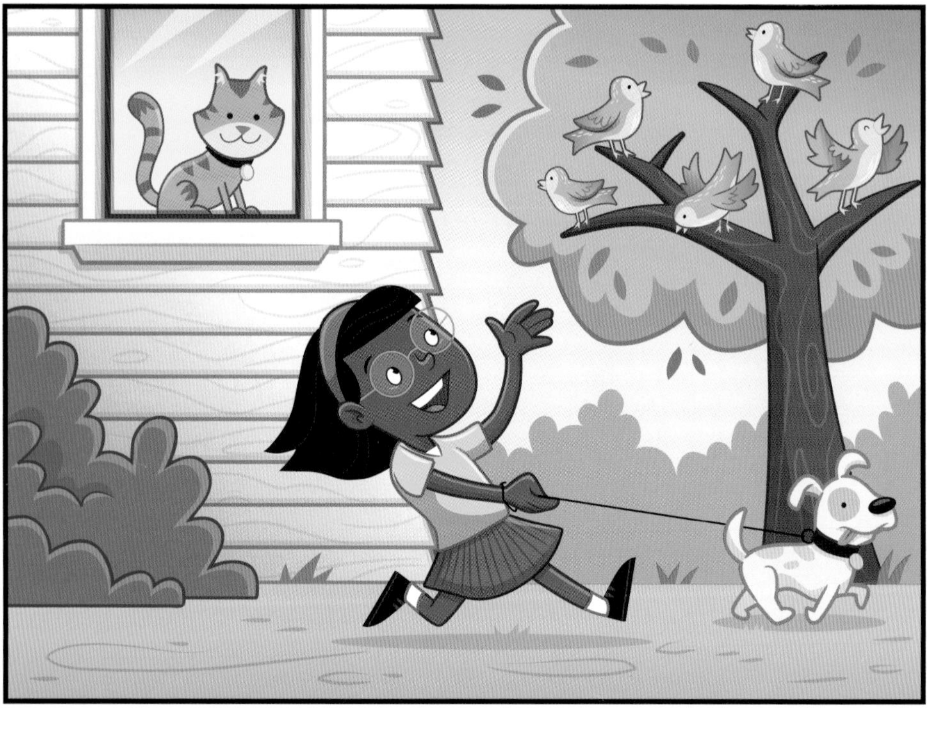

Migrating birds sometimes fly into windows. Tape pictures to windows to help birds see the glass.

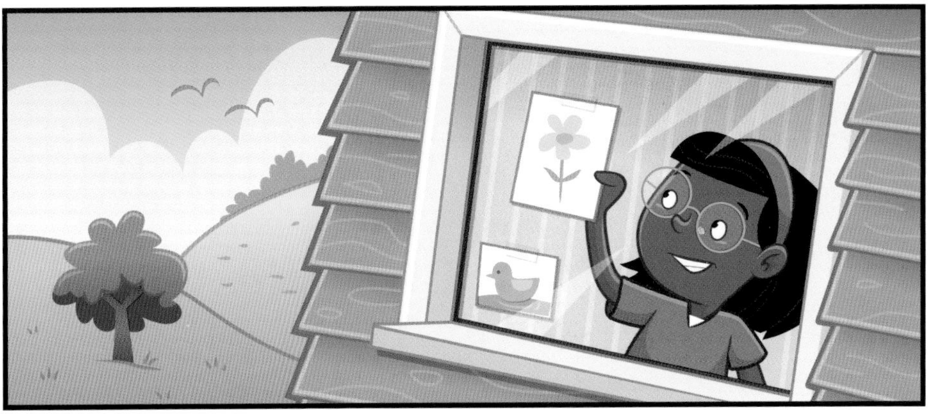

Birds face many dangers during migration. You can help them reach their summer and winter homes safely.

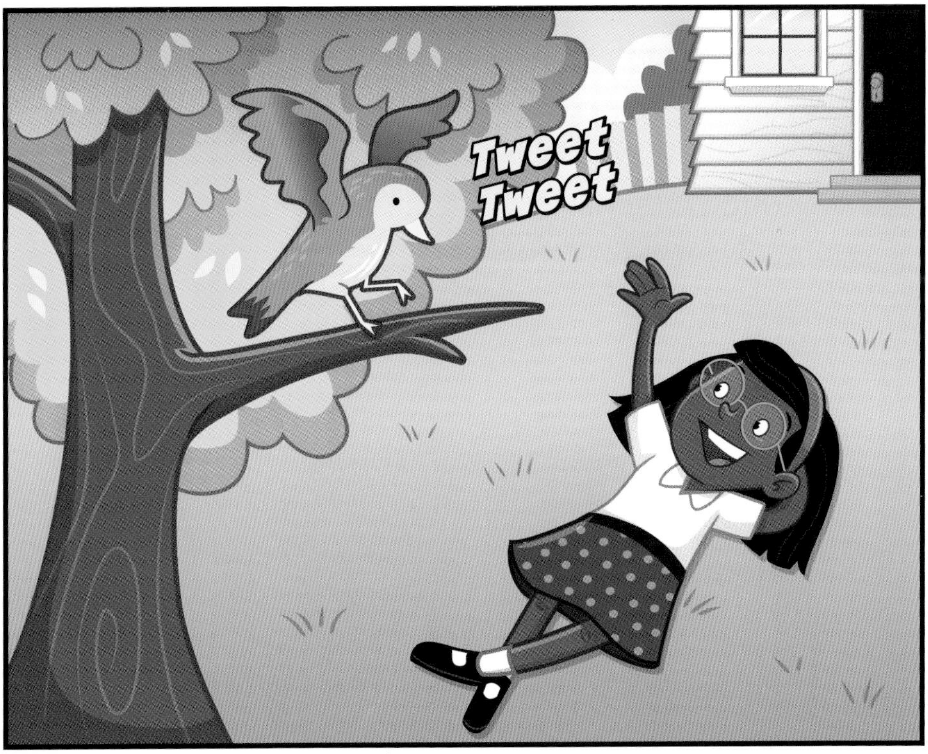
Tweet
Tweet

# GLOSSARY

**energy**—the strength to do active things without getting tired

**landmark**—an object that marks a route or a place

**magnet**—a piece of metal that attracts iron or steel

**magnetic field**—the area around a magnet that has the power to attract magnetic metals such as iron

**migration**—the seasonal movement of animals between summer and winter habitats

**sense**—to feel or be aware of something

# READ MORE

**Kalman, Bobbie.** *Why Do Animals Migrate?* Big Science Ideas. New York: Crabtree Pub., 2009.

**Nelson, Robin.** *Migration.* First Step Nonfiction. Discovering Nature's Cycles. Minneapolis: Lerner, 2011.

**O'Donnell, Liam.** *Amazing Animal Journeys.* DK Readers. 3, Reading Alone. New York: DK Pub., 2008.

# INTERNET SITES

FactHound offers a safe, fun way to find Internet sites related to this book. All of the sites on FactHound have been researched by our staff.

Here's all you do:

Visit *www.facthound.com*

Type in this code: 9781429660969

 **Super-cool stuff!** Check out projects, games and lots more at **www.capstonekids.com**

# INDEX

# SCIENCE MYSTERIES

## TITLES IN THIS SET:

**HOW DO WE KNOW ABOUT DINOSAURS?**
A FOSSIL MYSTERY

**HOW DO WE STAY ON EARTH?**
A GRAVITY MYSTERY

**WHERE DO THE BIRDS GO?**
A MIGRATION MYSTERY

**WHERE DOES THE SUN GO AT NIGHT?**
AN EARTH SCIENCE MYSTERY